LET'S
see

Kwanzaa

by Marc Tyler Nobleman

Content Adviser: Alton Hornsby Jr., Ph.D.,
Fuller E. Callaway Professor of History, Morehouse College, Atlanta, Georgia

Reading Adviser: Susan Kesselring, M.A., Literacy Educator,
Rosemount-Apple Valley-Eagan (Minnesota) School District

Let's See Library
Compass Point Books
Minneapolis, Minnesota

Compass Point Books
3109 West 50th Street, #115
Minneapolis, MN 55410

Visit Compass Point Books on the Internet at *www.compasspointbooks.com*
or e-mail your request to *custserv@compasspointbooks.com*

On the cover: The seven symbols of Kwanzaa

Photographs ©: Corbis, cover; Esbin-Anderson/Photo Network, 4; Maulana Karenga, Kwanzaa: A Celebration of Family, Community and Culture. Los Angeles: University of Sankore Press, 2002., 6; Francis Miller/Time Life Pictures/Getty Images, 8; Aneal Vohra/Index Stock Imagery, 10; John Burke/Index Stock Imagery, 12; Aneal F. Vohra/Unicorn Stock Photos, 14; Comstock, 16; Tom McCarthy/Photo Network, 18; Stephen Chernin/Getty Images, 20.

Creative Director: Terri Foley
Managing Editor: Catherine Neitge
Editors: Brenda Haugen and Christianne Jones
Photo Researcher: Marcie C. Spence
Designers: Melissa Kes and Les Tranby
Educational Consultant: Diane Smolinski

Library of Congress Cataloging-in-Publication Data
Nobleman, Marc Tyler.
    Kwanzaa / by Marc Tyler Nobleman.
        v. cm. — (Let's see)
    Includes bibliographical references and index.
Contents: What is Kwanzaa?—Who created Kwanzaa?—Why was Kwanzaa created?—What happens on Kwanzaa?—What are the seven principles of Kwanzaa?—What are the seven main symbols of Kwanzaa?—What are other traditions of Kwanzaa?—What is important at Kwanzaa?—What does Kwanzaa mean to people?
ISBN 0-7565-0647-6 (hardcover)
1. Kwanzaa—Juvenile literature. 2. African Americans—Social life and customs—Juvenile literature.
[1. Kwanzaa. 2. African Americans—Social life and customs. 3. Holidays.] I. Title. II. Series.
GT4403.A2N63 2005
394.2612—dc22   2003023623

Table of Contents

NOTE: In this book, words that are defined in the glossary
are in **bold** the first time they appear in the text.

What Is Kwanzaa?

Kwanzaa is a holiday that celebrates African **culture.** This holiday started in the United States. It honors African history, family, and **traditions.**

Kwanzaa lasts for seven days. It goes from December 26 to January 1.

Most schools, post offices, banks, government offices, and companies in the United States do not close for Kwanzaa. During this time, however, many people whose **ancestors** came from Africa think about their history and their future.

Who Created Kwanzaa?

Dr. Maulana Karenga created Kwanzaa in 1966. He was born in 1941 in the United States. He is a teacher, writer, and **activist.**

Dr. Karenga thought a holiday for black people would make them excited about their history. He believed they would enjoy learning about their past. He hoped they would keep sharing their history with younger people.

Dr. Karenga started **customs** for Kwanzaa. The customs were based on the **harvest** festivals from different African groups. The holiday of Kwanzaa was new, but its traditions were from long ago.

◀ *Dr. Maulana Karenga*

Why Was Kwanzaa Created?

Dr. Karenga wanted black people to think about their African ancestors. He wanted to bring families and communities together. Dr. Karenga wanted African-Americans to learn good **values** from their past. He wanted people to learn about African ways of life. He thought Kwanzaa would help keep people of African **descent** strong.

In the 1960s, black people worked hard to gain equality during the **civil rights movement.** Dr. Karenga thought about their courage when he made Kwanzaa.

◄ *People marched for equal rights for everyone in the 1960s.*

What Happens on Kwanzaa?

Kwanzaa is a family and community holiday. Relatives and friends gather to celebrate. They meet at home and in community buildings.

People tell stories and talk about the seven principles during each day of Kwanzaa. A principle is a rule that helps you know how to act in a good way. There is one principle for each day of Kwanzaa.

The seven principles of Kwanzaa are unity, self-determination, collective work and responsibility, cooperative economics, purpose, creativity, and faith. People talk about these principles during Kwanzaa, but they try to live by them all year long.

◄ *A Kwanzaa storyteller talks to his audience.*

What Do the Seven Principles of Kwanzaa Mean?

Unity is the first principle. This means staying together as a family and as a community. The principle of self-determination means being who you want to be. Collective work and responsibility means people should work together and help one another. For cooperative economics, a family may work together to save money for something the whole family wants or needs.

The principle of purpose means there is a reason for a person's actions. For creativity, people should use their talents and do their best. The last principle, faith, is believing in yourself and others.

◀ *A man talks with his family about Kwanzaa.*

What Are the Seven Main Symbols of Kwanzaa?

Symbols are objects that stand for something else. There are seven main symbols of Kwanzaa.

Crops stand for the African harvest. Crops may be fruits, vegetables, or nuts. The straw mat represents African tradition. The candleholder is a symbol that stands for African ancestors. Corn stands for the children of the family.

The seven candles represent the principles of Kwanzaa. The unity cup reminds people of the first principle of Kwanzaa—unity. The seventh symbol is gifts. The gifts show the love between parents and children.

◄ *The seven symbols of Kwanzaa*

What Are Other Traditions of Kwanzaa?

On each day of Kwanzaa, families light one candle in the candleholder. They talk about that day's principle. On the last day of Kwanzaa, they give gifts to one another.

Some people display the flag of the African **continent.** The flag's colors are red, black, and green. The red reminds people of how they have struggled. The black represents the African people. The green represents the land and the future.

On the last night of Kwanzaa, families join together for a feast. Many sing, dance, tell stories, or pray. Some people wear traditional African clothes.

◀ *A family gathers to light a candle.*

What Is Important at Kwanzaa?

Kwanzaa began in the United States, but it has helped bring together people in other countries, too. Kwanzaa is a holiday that many celebrate, no matter where they come from, where they live, or what their religion is.

Tradition is important at Kwanzaa. People eat, talk, and enjoy Kwanzaa customs. Some of these customs have been part of African culture for hundreds of years. It is a happy celebration.

During Kwanzaa, people give thanks for their blessings. They learn about their past. They use what they learn to make a good future for their families, their communities, and themselves.

◄ *A family celebrates by having a special meal.*

What Does Kwanzaa Mean to People?

Millions of people celebrate Kwanzaa each year. During this time, people think about how they are living their lives. They think about their communities, too. The holiday happens at the end of the year. People decide what they can try to do better next year.

During Kwanzaa, many black people all around the world take pride in their history. Together they have made it through tough times. Kwanzaa reminds them they are all connected. It reminds them there is always something to celebrate.

◄ *Members of a dance group perform an African dance.*

Glossary

activist—a person who works to make a problem better

ancestors—a person's grandparents, great-grandparents, and so on

civil rights movement—in the 1950s and 1960s, an effort to gain African-Americans equal treatment in the United States

continent—one of the seven large land areas on Earth; they are Africa, Antarctica, Asia, Australia, Europe, North America, and South America

culture—a group of people's beliefs, customs, and way of life

customs—things that members of a group usually do

descent—the family a person comes from

harvest—the time when crops are picked and gathered

traditions—customs that are common among a family or group

values—beliefs and ideas about what is important in life

Did You Know?

✴ The number seven is important during Kwanzaa. Kwanzaa has seven days, seven principles, seven symbols, and seven letters in its name.

✴ The word *Kwanzaa* comes from the Swahili phrase *matunda ya kwanza,* which means "first fruits." Swahili is the most widely spoken African language.

✴ You do not have to have African ancestors to enjoy Kwanzaa. It is a great chance to learn about African culture, just as you might learn about Chinese culture around the Chinese New Year or Mexican culture around Cinco de Mayo.

Want to Know More?

In the Library

Hintz, Martin, and Kate Hintz. *Kwanzaa: Why We Celebrate It the Way We Do.* Mankato, Minn.: Capstone Press, 1996.

Hoyt-Goldsmith, Diane. *Celebrating Kwanzaa.* New York: Holiday House, 1993.

Saint James, Synthia. *The Gifts of Kwanzaa.* Morton Grove, Ill.: A. Whitman, 1994.

Schaefer, Lola M. *Kwanzaa.* Mankato, Minn.: Pebble Books, 2001.

On the Web

For more information on *Kwanzaa,* use FactHound to track down Web sites related to this book.

1. Go to *www.facthound.com*
2. Type in a search word related to this book or this book ID: 0756506476.
3. Click on the *Fetch It* button.

Your trusty FactHound will fetch the best Web sites for you!

On the Road

The DuSable Museum of African American History
740 E. 56th Place
Chicago, IL 60637
773/947-0600
To learn about black history and see African-American art

The California African American Museum
600 State Drive
Exposition Park
Los Angeles, CA 90037
213/744-7432
To learn about black history and culture.

The flag of the African continent, The Bendera

Index

About the Author
Marc Tyler Nobleman has written more than 40 books for young readers. He has also written for a History Channel show called "The Great American History Quiz" and for several children's magazines including *Nickelodeon, Highlights for Children,* and *Read* (a Weekly Reader publication). He is also a cartoonist, and his single panels have appeared in more than 100 magazines internationally. He lives in Connecticut.